by Janet Alfieri and Ed Colley

Andrews and McMeel
A Universal Press Syndicate Company
Kansas City

ISBN: 0-8362-1891-4
Library of Congress Catalog Card Number: 92-70020

RETURN WITH US NOW TO THE FURTHERMOST OUTSKIRTS OF SUBURBIA...

A FIERY BRONCO... WITH THE SPEED OF LIGHT...

...A CLOUD OF DUST AND A HEARTY...

HI-HO, 7-ELEVEN, AWAY!

I WISH WE LIVED IN THE CITY.

THERE ARE NO MUSEUMS IN THE SUBURBS. NO GOURMET RESTAURANTS OR THEATERS OR CONCERTS.

FACE IT, MAX. WE LIVE IN A CULTURAL WASTELAND.

I TAKE IT, DARLENE, THAT YOU DIDN'T ENJOY "SALUTE TO WAYNE NEWTON NIGHT" AT THE VFW HALL.

DO YOU KNOW HOW I CAN TELL WHO MY BEST FRIENDS ARE, DARLENE?

NO, MAX. HOW?

WHEN GOOD FRIENDS COME TO VISIT... I DON'T RUN AROUND TRYING TO CLEAN UP THE HOUSE.

I AM REALLY TOUCHED, MAX.

5

7

18

SUBURBAN COWGIRLS

BY J. ALFIERI AND E. COLLEY

LOOK, DARLENE. AN INVITATION TO MY 20TH REUNION.

I SURE HOPE IT'S FROM MY ELEMENTARY SCHOOL.

SO ARE YOU GOING TO GO TO YOUR REUNION, MAX?

WELL, IF I CAN GET A SITTER FOR THE KIDS...

AND DROP AT LEAST FIFTEEN POUNDS OFF MY THIGHS...

BUY A DRESS THAT MAKES ME LOOK LIKE KIM BASINGER...

LAND AN IMPRESSIVE JOB AS A NETWORK ANCHORWOMAN...

START DATING EITHER HARRISON FORD OR KEVIN COSTNER...

AND MAKE "PEOPLE" MAGAZINE'S LIST OF THE TEN SEXIEST WOMEN IN AMERICA...

ONLY THEN, DARLENE, WILL I CONSIDER GOING.

WELL, IN THAT CASE, I'LL BABY-SIT.

23

24

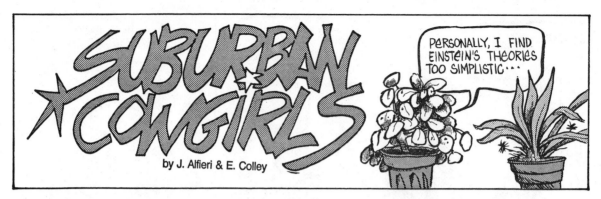

SUBURBAN COWGIRLS

BY J. ALFIERI AND E. COLLEY

HUT, TWO, THREE, FOUR!...

WE WILL SHOP UNTIL WE'RE SORE!

KEEP THOSE HEADS HIGH, AVOID ALL EYE CONTACT AND CLUTCH THOSE PURSES CLOSE TO YOUR CHESTS.

REMEMBER, URBAN SHOPPING IS NOT FOR THE FAINTHEARTED.

IT'S A FAR CRY FROM THOSE WIMPY SHOPPING MALLS YOU'RE ACCUSTOMED TO.

MAXINE! STEP FORWARD AND TELL THE CLASS WHERE THE DRESSING ROOMS IN BLOOM AND TAYLOR'S BARGAIN CELLAR ARE LOCATED!

ANYWHERE YOU CAN FIND ENOUGH SPACE TO TRY ON CLOTHES.

CORRECT!

DARLENE! WHAT DO YOU DO IF SOMEONE ON THE STREET ASKS FOR DIRECTIONS?

ALFIERI COLLEY

TELL THEM TO GET LOST, MA'AM.

RIGHT! ACT LIKE A NATIVE.

REMEMBER! WE ARE TOUGH! WE ARE STREETWISE! WE ARE LEAN, MEAN SHOPPING MACHINES! LET ME HEAR YOU SHOUT IT OUT LOUD!

THAT'S RIGHT!!!! WE'RE BAD!!!!

A FEW GOOD WOMEN

34

36

38

42

45

AS GOD IS MY WITNESS, I'LL NEVER FORGET TO BUY COFFEE AGAIN!

GET ME A COFFEE, WILL YOU?

WMOM RADIO

MAX, YOU WOULDN'T HAVE ASKED ME TO GET YOU COFFEE IF I WERE A WOMAN.

NO, DWAYNE. IF YOU WERE A WOMAN...

I'D EXPECT YOU TO READ MY MIND.

OUR GUEST TODAY IS JULIA WOLFE, GHOSTWRITER OF THE STARS.

JULIA, I SEE YOU HELPED DAN QUAYLE WRITE HIS LIFE STORY.

WAS THE VICE PRESIDENT DIFFICULT TO WORK WITH?

NO.

NOT ONCE HE UNDERSTOOD THAT AN AUTOBIOGRAPHY WASN'T A BOOK ABOUT CARS.

48

50

SUBURBAN COWGIRLS

BY J. ALFIER AND E. COLLEY

OH, NO!

ROBIN

MY CAT'S A NIP HEAD.

SNIFF! SNIFF!

ROBIN, DO YOU HAVE ANY IDEA WHAT THIS CATNIP STUFF CAN DO TO YOU?

HERE, TAKE A LOOK AT THIS.

THIS IS A NORMAL CAT.

NORMAL CAT

NOTICE THE CLEAR EYES, THE SHINY FUR AND THE GOOD POSTURE.

NOW HERE IS A CAT ON CATNIP.

SEE THE BUGGED OUT EYES, THE ARCHED BACK AND THE SIZZLING PAWS.

SIZZLING PAWS? HOLD IT! THIS ISN'T A CAT ON CATNIP.

THIS IS A CAT ON A HOT TIN ROOF.

SUBURBAN ★ COWGIRLS

BY J. ALFIERI AND E. COLLEY

GUESS WHAT DAY IT IS, DARLENE!

NATIONAL HEAD INJURY PREVENTION DAY?

ITS SUPER SSSUUUNNDDAAYYY!!!

SUNNNN-DAYYYY! FOR ONE DAY ONLY AT THE TAMPA TERRORDOME! SUNNNNDAYYYYY!

SEE THE FINAL BATTLE OF THE PRINCES OF PIGSKIN!

WITNESS THE BIZARRE RITUALS OF THE FRENZIED FANS!

HEAR THE CRUNCH OF COLLIDING BODIES, THE GRUNTS OF LEVIATHAN LINEMEN, THE BABBLE OF THE INANE SPORTSCASTERS!

IT'S SSSSSUUUUNNNN-DAYYYY!

AND I THOUGHT YOU DIDN'T UNDERSTAND!

60

SUBURBAN COWGIRL
BY J. ALFIERI AND E. COLLEY

THANKS, IGGY, BUT I THINK I'LL SIT THIS ONE OUT.

THAT LAST LAMBADA REALLY DID ME IN.

CATCH YOU LATER, EH?

AND, HEY, I HOPE THOSE VOICES YOU KEEP HEARING STOP REAL SOON.

IT'S A GOOD THING YOU AREN'T NATIVE AMERICAN, MAX.

WHY'S THAT, DARLENE?

YOUR INDIAN NAME WOULD BE "DANCES WITH JERKS."

ALFIERI COLLEY

64

SUBURBAN COWGIRLS
BY J. ALFIERI AND E. COLLEY

Gee, it must be a slow news week.

Thank you for shopping at Rick's Upscale Supermarket.

My name is Tanya and I'm your check-out person this evening.

Our specials today are fresh, organically grown broccoli clusters...

...Mother Jones hickory flavored tofu dogs...

...and oat bran pita bread, baked daily on the premises.

Would you like me to ring out your order now?

Could you, please, Tanya?

My Frusen Glädjé is getting soft.

68

SUBURBAN COWGIRLS

BY J. ALFIERI AND E. COLLEY

DOES ANYONE HAVE ANYTHING TO SHARE?

I HAVE A FEW BREATH MINTS HERE.

WELCOME TO THE PARENTS WITHOUT A CLUE SUPPORT GROUP.

WE ARE A FELLOWSHIP OF CONFUSED AND BAFFLED PARENTS SEEKING TO FIND OUR OWN PATHS THROUGH THE JUNGLE OF CHILD REARING.

WOULD ANYONE LIKE TO SHARE A PROBLEM OR CONCERN?··· MAXINE?

I'M REALLY WORRIED ABOUT THE SCHOOL VACATION COMING UP NEXT WEEK.

LAST YEAR, DURING MY KIDS' WINTER VACATION, I BECAME SO DISTRAUGHT I ATTEMPTED TO JOIN A CLOISTERED CONVENT.

ALFIERI COLLEY

I WAS READY TO TAKE A VOW OF SILENCE JUST TO GET A LITTLE PEACE AND QUIET.

ACTUALLY, IF IT WEREN'T FOR THEIR NO-TWINKIE VOW, I'D BE THERE TODAY.

SISTER MAXINE

SUBURBAN COWGIRLS

BY ALFIERI AND E. COLLEY

WELCOME TO THE FIFTH ANNUAL SUBURBAN COWGIRLS SPRING FASHION SHOW

THIS YEAR OUR SHOW IS ENTITLED "STRESS FOR SUCCESS."

OUR FIRST MODEL IS MAXINE MARSHAL, MOTHER OF TWO AND DEEJAY ON WMOM-FM.

MAX IS WEARING A LOVELY, DOUBLE-BREASTED POWER SUIT DESIGNED TO FIT THE NEEDS OF TODAY'S LOW-MAINTENANCE WOMAN.

NOTE THE PROVOCATIVE AND PRACTICAL SLIT-STYLE SKIRT WITH THE MONEY-SAVING, EXPANDING WAISTBAND.

MADE OF DURABLE, STAIN-RESISTANT, PERMA-PRESS FABRIC, THIS SUIT IS AVAILABLE IN A WIDE ARRAY OF CONSERVATIVE COLORS.

BUT WAIT! THE BEST IS YET TO COME!

WHEN MAX FEELS TENSION BUILDING AT THE OFFICE...

SHE JUST PUSHES THE BOTTOM BUTTON ON HER JACKET.

AND VOILA! VIBRATING SHOULDER PADS!!!

WHRRR!

WHRRR!

OOOH!

AAAH!

ALFIERI COLLEY

79

80

85

SUBURBAN COWGIRLS

BY J. ALFIERI AND E. COLLEY

I KNOW IT'S IN HERE SOMEWHERE.

THE STOPDUST SPRAY!

I SHOULD REALLY GIVE THIS PLACE A GOOD CLEANING.

I SHOULD DUST AND POLISH ALL THE FURNITURE.

I SHOULD GET DOWN ON MY HANDS AND KNEES AND SCRUB EVERYTHING WITH LOTS OF PINE-SCENTED CLEANER AND ELBOW GREASE.

I SHOULD USE A TOOTHBRUSH TO GET INTO ALL THOSE LITTLE CREVICES WHERE DISGUSTING THINGS HAVE BEEN COLLECTING FOR YEARS.

I GUESS YOU'LL BE BUSY FOR THE REST OF THE WEEK, MAX.

OH, I SAID I SHOULD DO THAT STUFF.

I HAVE NO INTENTION OF ACTUALLY DOING IT.

MOTHERS OF INTENTION

ALFIERI COLLEY

95

96

101

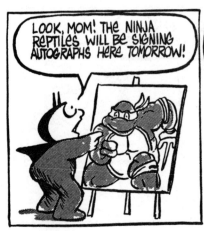

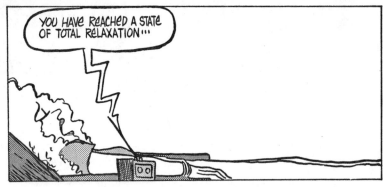

110

SUBURBAN COWGIRLS

BY J. ALFIERI AND E. COLLEY

MAXINE MARSHALL
LEAGUE'S LOWEST SCORING BOWLER

AND PROUD OF IT, MAN!

MAX, ITS YOUR TURN.

GET UP HERE NOW, MAX!

DID YOU KNOW ROSEANNE ONCE THREATENED A PHOTOGRAPHER WITH A BOWLING BALL?

ALIENS INVADE K-MART

LOOK! EVERYONE! I DIDN'T GET A GUTTER BALL! I ACTUALLY KNOCKED SOME PINS DOWN!

I AM SO PSYCHED! DO YOU THINK I CAN GET A STRIKE NEXT TIME?

MAX? THIS IS BOWLING! REMEMBER?

THE SPORT YOU ONCE CALLED THE STUPIDEST PASTIME ON EARTH NEXT TO MACRAME.

BUT THAT WAS BEFORE I EXPERIENCED THE THRILL OF VICTORY!

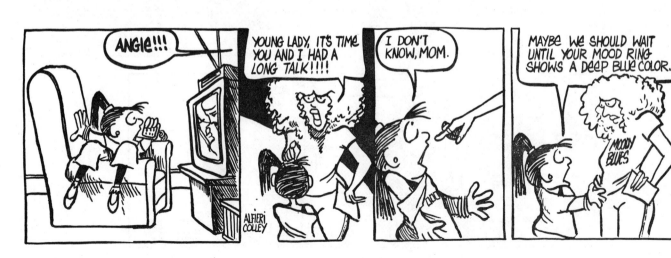

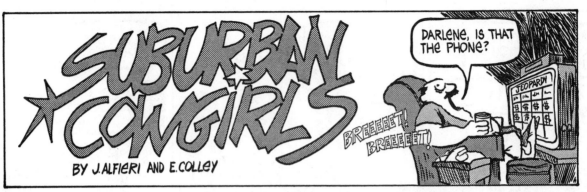

SUBURBAN COWGIRLS

BY J. ALFIERI AND E. COLLEY

WAR IS HECK!

IRAQ

IT INTERRUPTS REGULARLY SCHEDULED PROGRAMS.

LET'S PLAY WAR!

YES!!

WE'LL BE THE AMERICANS AND YOU GUYS BE THE REPUBLICAN GUARD!

NO, WE'RE THE AMERICANS!

NO, US!

US!

HOLD IT... WE CAN ALL BE AMERICANS...

WE'LL PLAY CIVIL WAR!

126